Mama's pearls of guidance

One mama's lullaby
to her beloved son.
Snuggle, laugh &
sing along!

Written By Lisa Marie Gilbert
Illustrated By Lorraine Shulba

First Edition
Published by Blazon International Ltd.
Calgary, AB
www.blazoninternational.ca

Graphic Design, Cover Design by Lorraine Shulba www.bluebugstudios.com
Library and Archives Canada Cataloguing in Publication
Gilbert, Lisa Marie, author
Mama's Pearls of Guidance / written by Lisa Marie Gilbert;
Illustrated by Lorraine Shulba www.lorraineshulba.com

Issued in print format
ISBN: 978-1-7778027-2-1

Text and illustration Copyright 2022 Lisa Marie Gilbert
Author photo credit: Valerie McIntyre Photography

All rights reserved. No part of this publication may be reproduced, stored in a retrieval system, or transmitted in any form or by any means – electronic, mechanical, photocopying, and recording or otherwise – without prior written permission from the author. The exception would be brief passages by a reviewer in a newspaper or magazine or online. To perform any of the above is an infringement of copyright law.

Collect the Mama's series! Also available from author Lisa Marie Gilbert:
Mama's Words of Wisdom
Mama's Pearls of Guidance
Mama's Girl Guide to Believing in Yourself

For more information about the author, her books, and products, visit:
www.lisamarie-gilbert.com
www.facebook.com/lisamariegilbertwriter
www.instagram.com/lisagilbert_author

To my River Baby Love "Moonlight"
Our answered prayer.
Our love and strength you cannot mistake,
Our Gilbert Ring you will never break.
Our family circle is complete.

Thank you for showing me the way back home,
You will forever be the light on my water.
Love Mama ox

And for Ricky, "my brother from another mother".
I love you and will always have your back,
thank you for always having mine.

Mama's answered prayer,
From heaven above,
God sent me you
My miracle baby love.

Oh Mr. Giggles how you make me chuckle
Just what the world needs -
More laughing and loving without a care
You are so my smiley, wily sunshine bear.

I look forward all the day long
To holding you tight, slow dancin' to our song,
Snugglin' and huggin', saying bye-bye to the day
Let's meet in Dreamland –
dinos and dragons can show us the way.

You're the best – there's no denying that
Pay attention to what's in the world around
Never take people or things you love for granted
Keep your feet on the ground.

Do onto others as you'd have done to yourself
Always an important lesson to recall,
Be thoughtful and remember others' feelings
If it is not kind don't say it at all.

For your words do matter
Make the choice to be nice
People will smile as you walk away
And in turn, the universe
will reward you one day.

So many decisions on the rollercoaster of life
is your glass half empty or is it half full?
Say goodbye to any gloomy darkness
Let all positive energy be your pull.

Have respect for all
Teachers, elders, friends, and fam
Especially your hardworking Mama
Please and thank you ma'am!

Remember your family – stay loyal and true
Your pals and gals will come and go
But we will always have your back,
Your Mama, your Dada, and your loving big Bro.

Remember to love yourself too
Try your best and set your goals high
Climb your mountain, I know you will
Your limit is the sky.

When I'm feeling down, your love lifts me up,
Glowing light on the water guides me home
My moonlight, my starbright,
my beautiful perfect poem.

No two are alike, follow your own true path
We all are different for a reason
Stand up for you and others on the journey
For life would be boring with only one season

Winter summer spring or fall
What will your adventure bring?
Ups and downs, twists and turns
Greats and breaks for you my little king!

I love your style, I dig your song
Swingin' and singin'
Driftin' away with you I can't go wrong!

Mama's eternal wish - fill your life with song
From keys to guitars as long as you play -
Rhythm and rhyme will show you the way.

Magic carpet ride - where will it take you?
Laugh, cry, save your mortal soul
Rock you like a hurricane
Imagine Sergeant Pepper - that's how we roll.

Silly screams, LOL or rocking' to the band
Can be heard loud and clear across this great land
But turn it down my little clown and get ready for bed
Mama always says there's a time and place
for everything my little sleepy head.

To tell your story you must live your story

Travel the globe my worldly little man

First comes school, then experiencing life
While you jet set from Calgary to Japan.

Your heart and your sweetness
So pure and true
Your hugs are the best in the west
When I'm feeling blue.

Dream, dream, dream, dream
Dream until your dreams come true
Never give up my champion
Your Mama believes in you.

Special thanks to the Musical hero's and legends as mentioned in book. Listen to this playlist with your kids!

The Beatles, Let it Be, Apple Records, 1970 and "Sgt. Pepper's Lonely Hearts Club Band", EMI, 1967

Creedence Clearwater Revival (CCR), Susie-Q, Fantasy, 1968

Dobie Gray, Drift Away, Decca Records, 1973

Elton John, "Rocket Man – I Think It's Going to be a Long, Long Time", Honky Chateaû, Uni, 1972

Janis Joplin (also known as "Pearl")

John Lennon, Imagine, Apple Records, 1971

Don McLean, American Pie, United Artis Records, 1971

The Scorpions, "Rock You Like a Hurricane", Love at First Sting, Mercury, 1984

Steppenwolf, "Magic Carpet Ride", The Second, ABC Dunhill, 1968

Cat Stevens / Yusuf Islam

Rolling Stones

The WHO, Who are you?, MCA, 1978